Christian Signboard Quotes

Chewy One-liners!

Henry Jacob Rupp

ISBN: 1497465052
ISBN 13: 9781497465053

Sandy Robb Jane Jeremy
Kendra Jody Gabe Christy
Zachary Isaiah Henry
Jeremiah Selah Aowyn
Nyah Lydian

Preface

A signboard is always working, day in and day out without pay, to encourage people who pass by to seek the Lord. Always silent, but speaking loudly, each message seeks a response from the reader. Uplifting some days, challenging other days, the signboard is always worth reading.

Stressed and exhausted people passing by anticipate your signboard messages. These messages, accompanied by prayer, will do more for the Kingdom of God than you can imagine!

"THEREFORE, MY DEAR BROTHERS, STAND FIRM. LET NOTHING MOVE YOU. ALWAYS GIVE YOURSELVES FULLY TO THE WORK OF THE LORD, BECAUSE YOU KNOW THAT YOUR LABOR IS NOT IN VAIN." 1 Corinthians 15:58

Content

I

Advice

———

Be humble, be gentle. Ephesians 4:2

Love mercy, act justly and walk humbly with your God. Micah 6:8

This is the one I esteem; He who is humble, contrite, and trembles at my Word. Isaiah 66:2

Humble yourself before God; He will lift you up. James 4:10

If God's people will humble themselves, God will heal their land. 2 Chronicles 7:14

Follow Me! Jesus Matthew 9:9

Wait for the Lord; be strong and take heart. Psalm 27:14

Better to be poor than a liar. Proverbs 19:22

Don't lie - not good. Exodus 20:16

A man without God is like trusting in a spider web. Job 8:14

Hope in the Lord and soar like an eagle. Isaiah 40:31

Advice

Honor your parents and you will live long. Ephesians 6:1,2

Read God's life insurance policy in Romans 10.

Confess Jesus is Lord and you will be saved. Romans 10:9

Believe that God raised Jesus from the dead and you will be saved. Romans 10:9

Live in the House of the Lord forever. Psalm 23:6

Be attractive - adorn yourself with humility and gentleness. Ephesians 4:2

Press on to reach the Heavenly prize. Philippians 3:14

Be content with what you have. Hebrews 13:5

Draw near to God and He will draw near to you. James 4:8

Give thanks to the Lord for He is good. Psalm 106:1

Rejoice in the Lord always. Philippians 3:1

The first shall be last and the last shall be first. Matthew 19:30

Honor your Father and Mother and you will live long. Exodus 20:12

Love your neighbor as much as you love yourself. Matthew 22:39

The Truth will set you free! Jesus John 8:32

Don't hide your light under a bushel. Matthew 5:15

Seek the Lord while He may be found. Isaiah 55:6

Treat only God as God. Have no possessions above Him. Deuteronomy 5:7

Don't grieve the Holy Spirit of God. Ephesians 4:30

The beginning of wisdom is the fear of the Lord. Proverbs. 9:10

Taste and see that the Lord is good. Psalm 34:8

Open your mouth; God will fill it. Psalm 81:10

Do not wear yourself out to get rich; Have the wisdom to show restraint. Proverbs 23:4

Give thanks in all circumstances for this is the Will of God. 1Thessalonians 5:18

Delight in the Lord and He will give you the desires of your heart. Psalms 37:4

Seek God first and all these things will be added. Matthew 6:33

A gentle answer turns away wrath, but a harsh word stirs up anger. Proverbs 15:1

Be content with what you have. Hebrews 13:5

Seek first the Kingdom of God and His righteousness and all these things will be added. Matthew 6:33

For the happy heart - life is a continual feast. Proverbs 15:15

Contentment with Godliness makes you a very rich person. Timothy 6:6

Think about what is true and noble, right and pure. Philippians 4:8

Advice

A live dog is better than a dead lion. Enjoy life! Ecclesiastes 9:4

Self denial may give you your greatest joy. Hebrews 11:25

Don't put a question mark where God put a period.

If you suppress the Truth, you are without excuse.

The best way to save face is to keep the lower part shut.

You can't shake hands with a closed fist.

ANGER is only one letter from DANGER.

If you chase 2 rabbits, both will escape - seek God only.

Be yourself - everybody else is taken.

The best way to have the last word is to apologize.

Finish strong!

If a man needs praise - give it to him. He cannot read his tombstone.

Trust and obey - there is no other way.

Try moral beautification - I can help! Jesus

If the barn needs painting - paint it.

Sometimes the majority only means that all the fools are on the same side.

The straight and narrow path would not be so narrow if more people would walk on it.

Plan ahead - it wasn't raining when Noah built the Ark.

He who angers you controls you.

If you are happy, notify your face.

If you are going to blow a horn, blow a trumpet for God.

Is anything more important than eternity with God?

Modern culture is trying to mix all religions into one.

Google doesn't have all the answers! God

"In God We Trust" - The dollar has it correct.

If you doubt God, remember you don't have all the facts.

To hate is easy - to forgive is hard. Do something hard today!

Seek God - It's always open at the top.

Every day is Judgement Day - use a lot of it.

Laughter is a mini-vacation. Have many mini's this month.

Can't find God? call _____. We can help!

Take a "God Look" at yourself.

Don't waste your life! God

Do unto others as you would have them do to you.

Do unto others as though you were the others.

Advice

Rejoice in the Lord always, always, always.

What is greater than God? Nothing!

You can't change the past but you can ruin a perfectly good present by worrying about the future.

Do not face the day until you have faced God.

Listen to no man who has not listened to God.

If you are a man, be one.

He is no fool to give up that which he cannot keep to gain what he cannot lose. Jim Elliot

People are seldom too busy to stop and tell you how busy they are.

The only people you should get even with are those who helped you.

Watch your step! Everyone else does.

He who knows everything has a lot to learn.

When you are through improving, you are through.

The main thing about the main thing is that it is the main thing.

Always put off until tomorrow what you should not do at all.

After all is said and done, more is said than done.

Lord, help me to be the person my dog thinks I am.

Real friends are those who, when you feel you've made a fool of yourself, don't feel you've done a permanent job.

A mule makes no headway when he is kicking - neither does a man.

When you are in deep water, it's a good idea to keep your mouth shut.

One way to get ahead and stay ahead is to use your head.

He, who is good at making excuses, is seldom good for much else.

Nothing else ruins the truth like stretching it.

TV may be the thief in your house (life).

Don't let the littleness in others, bring out the littleness in you.

Don't boast when you should blush.

Don't make God angry at you - He's a lot bigger.

Do your best and then sleep in peace - God is awake.

II

Battle

The battle is the Lords. 1 Samuel 17:47

The battle is not yours but the Lord's. 2 Chronicles 20:15

Don't go into the spiritual battle naked - put on the Armor of God. Ephesians 6

Put on the Armor of God! Ephesians 6:11

The horse is made ready for the battle, but the victory belongs to the Lord. Proverbs 21:31

Fight the good fight of faith. 1 Timothy 6:12

The task ahead of us is never as great as the Power behind us.

Life on earth is really just bootcamp for Heaven.

We all are in a battle to know God. Win!

Is what you are living for worth dying for?

"Lord God Almighty" is found 57 times in the Bible.

In your battle with good and evil, always choose good.

Do mortal combat against sin.

God wins in the end.

Stones and sticks are thrown only at fruit-bearing trees.

The fruit is out on the limb.

God is in the end - don't jump ship.

Be a strong person.

The battle is not yours - it is the Lord's.

III

Bible

———

The Word of the Lord stands forever. 1 Peter 2:25

All Scripture is God breathed. 2 Timothy 3:16

Delight in God's Word. Psalm 1:2

The Bible is a light for your path. Psalm 119:105

Memorize Scripture in your heart. Psalm 119:11

Let the Truth set you free! Jesus John 8:32

I will instruct you and teach you in the way you should go. Psalms 32:8

The Bible may cause you to wonder, but never to wander.

The Bible will not be a dry book if you know the author.

Long lasting relief is not found in a bottle but in the Bible.

Every answer is found in the Bible.

Bible - God's Supernatural Book.

Culture does not change the Bible.

The Bible says what it means and means what it says.

The Bible has been a greater force for good than any other book ever.

The Bible is one book that has never been proven wrong.

B I B L E - Basic Instructions Before Leaving Earth.

The Bible has all the answers to all the problems. Ronald Reagan

The key to happiness is found in the Bible.

Have you read my best seller? God

It takes only 78 hours to read the entire Bible! Start today.

There are still many free gifts in the Bible for you.

Be in the Word more than the world.

If we don't change the message, the message can change us.

Read the Bible - it will scare the Hell out of you.

The future is as bright as the Promises of God.

We don't change God's Message - His Message changes us.

IV

Choice

Everyone who calls on the Name of the Lord will be saved. Romans 10:13

Delight in God's Word. Psalm 1:2

Delight in the Lord - He will give you your desires. Psalm 37:4

Commit your way to God - He will bring it to pass. Psalm 37:5

Call upon God! He will answer you. Jeremiah 33:3

Rejoice in the Lord always. Philippians 3:1

Be strong in the Lord and in His mighty power. Ephesians 6:10

Choose to serve God. Joshua 24:15

If you seek God, you will find God. Jeremiah 29:13

Seek God and get right with Him and everything else will be added. Matthew 6:33

Enter the narrow gate. It's worth it. Matthew 7:13

Treat only God as God - have no possessions above Him. Deuteronomy 5:7

Don't misuse the Name of God; He remembers. Exodus 20:7

Ask and you will be given; seek and you will find. Matthew 7:7

Work out your salvation with fear and trembling. Philippians 2:12

Give thanks in all circumstances for this is the Will of God. 1 Thessalonians 5:17

Rejoice always and again I say rejoice. Philippians 4:4

Seek first the Kingdom of God and His righteousness and all these things will be added. Matthew 6:33

If you truly seek Me, you will surely find Me, says the Lord. Jeremiah 29:13

Give thanks to the Lord for He is good; His love endures forever. Psalm 118:1

Stand firm in the faith - do everything in love. 1 Corinthians 16:13,14

Be patient. James 5:7

Do unto others as you want them to do to you. Matthew 7:12

He who will not sail until he has favorable winds will lose many a voyage. Proverbs 19:3

Encourage the weak; be patient with everyone. 1 Thessalonians 5:14

Resist Satan in God's power and Satan will flee from you. James 4:7

Come near to God and He will come near to you. James 4:8

Choice

Return to Me and I will return to you, says the Lord Almighty. Malachi 3:7

Travel steadily along His path. Psalm 37:34

Think about what is true and noble, right and pure. Philippians 4:8

Finally brothers, whatever is true, noble, right, pure, lovely, admirable - if anything is excellent and praiseworthy, think about such things. Philippians 4:8

Welcome! Jesus Matthew 14:29

L ife is short - seek God hard while He may be found.

What you do today matters for eternity.

Your parents' faith won't work for you.

Go with God! He will be with you to the ends of the earth.

Be saved, safe and satisfied.

Come agnostic - leave Christian.

Come athiest - leave Christian.

The ultimate self denial is atheism.

There is no good reason not to follow Jesus.

You have a chance to make a difference - do it.

Don't miss Heaven for the world.

Your life is a test from God. Are you passing?

Don't ignore God.

Ask Jesus to be Lord of your life.

Not trusting in the Lord is a terrible disease.

Men - step up to the plate! Jesus.

Don't settle for less than God's highest and best.

We are who we hang around. Hang around Jesus.

Don't fear dying - rather fear not having lived.

Bathe always in gratitude to God.

God always wins - keep close on His side.

You will take your character into eternity, not your career.

Being satisfied in God is our calling and our duty.

Seek your own joy in the joy of your spouse.

Pursue true joy. Seek God.

Seek God hard while He may be found.

God doesn't accept excuses - there is plenty of evidence.

You are here for a purpose. Live it. Jesus

If you don't live it, you don't believe it.

Nothing worth keeping is lost in serving God.

Choice

Most people are trying to become less dependent on God. God is trying to help people be more dependent on Him.

Going my way? God

Salvation is free, but not until you ask for it.

Do the right thing - you will please some people and astonish the rest.

How to find Christianity? Turn right and keep moving.

Buddha's tomb - occupied. Mohammed's tomb - occupied. Jesus's tomb - empty! Why follow a loser?

It will cost you more to say "No" to God than to say "Yes".

Take a "God look" at yourself.

Trust and obey - there is no other way.

To be almost saved is to be totally lost.

Are you ready?

Life has many choices - eternity has two. What's yours?

What if God is asking us for a sign?

Heaven is a world of love - choose to go there.

God is the main thing!

Are you walking the talk?

Don't forfeit eternal rewards for temporary gains now.

Is anything more important than eternity with God?

If you are headed in the wrong direction, God allows "u-turns".

If you don't like the way you were born, try being born again.

In the dark? Follow the Son.

It costs nothing to become a Christian, but it costs everything to be a Christian.

If Christ is kept outside, something must be wrong inside.

Choose the Bread of Life or you are toast.

Self denial may give you your greatest joy.

If God is your co-pilot, switch seats.

Be an organ donor - give your heart to Jesus.

It's not how you start, it's how you finish that counts.

Man's way leads to a hopeless end - God's Way leads to an endless hope.

We set the sail - God makes the wind.

His Grace is your peace in the race.

The Will of God will never take you to where the Grace of God will not protect you.

Seek the Lord while He may be found.

Life is a 100 year vapor - think eternity.

Choice

Need eternal fire insurance?

If you died today, would you go to Heaven?

If you give God the chance, He will touch your soul.

Life is slippery. Here, take My hand! Jesus

To hate is easy - to forgive is hard. Do something hard.

To sin is human - to persist is idiocy.

In trying times, don't stop trying.

We are all invited to a Heavenly Feast but we must R.S.V.P.

Be a billboard for God.

Here I am Lord - send _____!

Two words never to say! "No Lord".

He who sows sparingly will reap sparingly.

Feed your faith and your doubts will starve to death.

Men do not fail. They give up trying.

If Christ is the Way, why waste time traveling another way?

Do not pray for an easy life - pray to be a strong person.

Don't condone what God condemns.

Every home is a school - what do you teach?

God loves everyone, but prefers "Fruits of the Spirit" over "religious nuts".

You can tell how big a person is by what it takes to discourage him.

Don't go into the spiritual battle naked. Put on the Armor of God!

Conversion is going into business with God.

Some people never get religion in their hands and feet.

Most people want to serve God, but only in an advisory capacity.

In trying times don't stop trying.

Are you a spiritual growth drop-out?

Don't get caught with the opposition! God

A hypocrite is a person who's not himself on Sunday.

Few love to hear of the sins they act.

If Christ is the Way, why waste time traveling another way?

What you really, really desire is what you worship!

V

Christ

———

The Lord is my Shepherd, I shall lack nothing. Psalm 23:1

Jesus is King of Kings and Lord of Lords! Revelation 19:16

My people recognize My voice. Jesus John 10:27

For the joy to save us, Jesus endured the Cross. Hebrews 12:2

Jesus is always with you. Matthew 28:20

Love never fails - Jesus loves you. 1 Corinthians 13:8

Christ in you - the Hope of Glory. Colossians 1:27

To live is Christ - to die is gain. Philippians 1:21

Jesus Christ is the only Way. John 14:6

God sent Jesus so that we won't perish! John 3:16

He who believes in Jesus shall live. John 11:25

Believe in Jesus Christ and be saved. Romans 10:9

The Message of the Cross is foolishness to some, but the power of God for those who are saved. 1 Corinthians 1:18

Jesus Christ is the same yesterday, today and forever. Hebrews 13:8

Jesus in you is stronger than Satan who is in the world. 1 John 4:4

No one who believes in Christ will ever be disappointed. Romans 10:11

In Christ you will become a new person. 2 Corinthians 5:17

Jesus is the Way - there is no other way. John 14:6

I have come to give you a more significant life. John 10:10

The ultimate macho man is Jesus - He took on the sins of the world.

There is infinite value in knowing Jesus Christ as Lord.

Jesus - The Lion of Judah.

Aslan (Jesus) is not a tame lion! Chronicles of Narnia

My peace I give to you. Jesus

If you put Jesus first, you will be happy at last.

Too much drama? Let Jesus set you free.

Jesus gets monkeys off people's backs.

Jesus is the answer!

Is Jesus your BFF? (best friend forever)

Christ

You love Jesus as much as the person you love least.

The humble carpenter of Nazareth was also the mighty Architect of the universe!

In this life, it's not what you have but Who you have that counts.

It is better to be with Christ in the storm than in smooth water without Him.

Come - I will give you rest! Jesus

Fear or anger problem? Jesus came to set you free.

Jesus Christ is our steering wheel - not our spare tire.

I have risen and I shall return soon. Jesus Christ

Jesus in you is stronger than any evil in the world.

When your back is against the wall, remember His was against the Cross.

Try moral beautification - I can help. Jesus

I love you so much! Jesus

I invite you to a better life! Jesus

I am the Way and the Truth! J C

We all need a Savior to do what no one else can do.

Jesus is coming soon.

Is the Son in your eye?

Jesus is the only one who can give you life happily ever after.

Jesus is also the mighty architect of the universe.

Jesus loves you and has a wonderful plan for your life.

Ask Jesus to be Lord of your life today!

Don't fear - Jesus is near.

When it's impossible, Jesus does His best work.

Jesus invested His life in you! Any interest yet?

Let Jesus change your misery into ministry.

Don't be caught dead without Jesus.

Come - I will give you rest! Jesus

Believe in the Lord Jesus Christ and be saved! Bible

Choose Jesus today! There is time.

Rejoice in the Lord always, always, always!

The main thing about the main thing is that it's the main thing. Jesus is the main thing.

Lets be close friends! Jesus

Make Jesus Christ Lord of your life and live forever.

Christ

He who rejects Me (Jesus), rejects Him who sent Me.

Never will I leave you; never will I forsake you! Jesus

Jesus' pain - your gain.

There is nothing greater than Jesus.

He hung for your hang ups.

I am the Bread of Life! Jesus

Keep cooking for Jesus.

I am the good Shepherd - Jesus

Jesus rescues people from ordinary life to get extraordinary life.

The Son of God became the Son of Man so that He might change the Sons of Men into the Sons of God.

Man's best friend, Jesus, has conquered man's worst enemy, death.

Jesus wants to be your breakthrough.

Need a life guard? Ours walks on water.

When facing the Son, you see no shadows.

Jesus is the Son of God! Believe in Him.

Are you ready? Jesus Christ

Life is slippery. Here, take My hand. Jesus

VI

Christians

———

If anyone is in Christ, he is a new person; the old has gone, the new has come. 2 Corinthians 5:17

The righteous are as bold as a lion. Proverbs 28:1

Jesus came so that you may have more abundant life. John 10:10

The Lord is my Shepherd, I shall lack nothing. Psalm 23:1

Precious in the sight of the Lord is the death of His Saints. Psalm 116:15

Be humble, be gentle. Ephesians 4:2

In Christ you will become a new person. 2 Corinthians 5:17

For your own sake, get saved! John 3:16

Non-believers should be able to see Christ in believers. 1 Corinthians 4:16

I am the Lord - those who hope in Me will never be disappointed. Isaiah 49:23

Memorize Scripture in your heart. Psalms 119:11

Christians

Crave spiritual food to grow up. 1 Peter 2:2

For the happy heart, life is a continual feast. Proverbs 15:5

Christians never meet for the last time!

Do people know that you are Christian by your love?

Many people use Christianity like a bus - they ride it only when it's going their way.

All Christians work for the same employer.

Everyone has beauty but not everyone sees it.

We must be winsome to win some for Christ.

Porcupine Christians have many good points but you cannot get close to them.

The Lord is my shepherd! Is He yours?

It is awesome to be a Christian.

Many people are on the salvation train, but a lot of them are in the sleeping car.

The true Christian is one who is right side up in an upside down world.

God doesn't call the qualified. He qualifies the called.

Three types of Christians - goers, senders, and disobedient.

Is what you are living for worth dying for?

If you love God more than your spouse, you will be married a long time.

Cowards - become Christians.

Disciples make disciples.

It is better to be Godly and poor, than rich and evil.

Redemption is God's recycling plan.

Salvation is free but not valid until you ask for it.

If Christ is kept outside, something must be wrong inside.

Are you an undercover Christian?

Christians, like pianos, need frequent tuning.

To be "meek" is to be like a well trained war horse.

The safest place to be is in the center of God's will.

Is there enough evidence out there to convict you of being a Christian?

If you were a billboard, what would the message of your life be to others?

He who is born of God is certain to resemble His Father.

Warm people make up for cold weather.

What you do today matters for eternity.

God has no grandchildren - only sons and daughters.

Love the lost, the last, and the least. Jesus

You are God's treasured possession - that's your best possession.

You are made in God's image. Don't misuse it.

Preach the Gospel at all times - use words if necessary.

Without solitude it is impossible to live a spiritual life.

The main thing God asks for is our attention.

We need "God Confidence" more than "self confidence".

Glorify God by enjoying Him forever.

Be a "GODAHOLIC".

The business of everyday is to prepare for our last day.

Everything we do teaches - don't cause others to sin.

Promote an attitude of gratitude.

Who is your good shepherd?

Be satisfied with a dissatisfied satisfaction.

Be satisfied with a dissatisfied satisfaction - be
hungry for God.

Be hungry for God.

God is jealous for your devotion.

A stranger is one away from home, but a pilgrim is one who is on his way home.

Keep your commitment to Christ at full strength.

I live to die, I die to live - the more I die, the more I live.

The truest end of life is to know the life that will never end.

Aspire to inspire before you expire.

You are here for a purpose - live it! Jesus

Jesus saves people from ordinary life to get them to extraordinary life.

God is jealous for your devotion.

Christians never meet for the last time.

Don't fear dying. Rather fear not having lived.

Most people want to serve God, but only in an advisory position.

God doesn't need great men, great men need God.

Be an organ donor - give your heart to Jesus.

All Christians work for the same employer.

You are on Heaven's most wanted list.

Be thankful to the One who filled your stockings with legs.

Put your hope in the Lord for Heaven's sake.

Seventy five percent of those who receive Christ as Savior do so by age 18.

Be attractive; adorn yourself with humility and gentleness. Ephesians 4:2

If the barn needs painting, paint it. God

He who lives well preaches well.

Those who fear the Lord lack no good thing.

Loved the wedding; invite Me to the marriage. God

That "love thy neighbor" thing. I meant it. God

God is jealous for your devotion.

You are here for a purpose - live it. Jesus Christ

To the world you might be one person, but to one person you might be the world.

If you don't live it, you don't believe it.

Believe me now, see me later. God

Man's best friend, Jesus, has conquered man's worst enemy, death.

It's not how you start, it's how you finish that counts.

Have you kept your promise to God?

Are you walking the talk?

There is no excess in the realm of spiritual appetite.

Christians, keep the faith - but not from others.

If you are going to blow a horn, blow a horn for God.

Those who honor and love God need not fear God's wrath.

Trust and obey - there's no other way.

Be hungry for God.

Go and make disciples of all nations. Jesus

What is your life about?

It's not about your happines - it is about your holiness.

VII

Church

Don't forsake meeting together as some are in the habit of doing. Hebrews 10:25

If your life stinks, we have a pew for you.

The church is a hospital for sinners - not a rest home for saints.

The fastest growing religion is "no religion".

Yes - we are open Sundays.

Need a friend? Welcome

CH_ _ CH What's missing? U R

Under same management for 2000 years.

Running low on faith? Stop in for a fill-up.

Want a trip to Heaven? See salesman inside church for details.

Faith comes by hearing the Word. Welcome

Soul food served here! Welcome

Let's meet at My house Sunday before the game! God

C'mon over and bring the kids! God

Having trouble sleeping? We have sermons; come and hear one.

Sign broken - message inside this Sunday.

Going to church does not make you a Christian anymore than going to Mcdonald's makes you a hamburger.

Free trip to Heaven - details inside.

Open Sundays.

If a sermon pricks your conscience, it must have some good points.

Don't wait for six strong men to take you to church.

Come early for a good back-seat.

Your Gramma's praying that you'll go to church. Might as well try this church.

VIII

Creation/Science

———

In the beginning God. Genesis 1:1

Nothing in all creation is hidden from God. Hebrews 4:13

God is in control. Revelation 19:6

S cience is the exploration of God's creation.

In the beginning God created everything out of nothing.

Nature is the art work of God.

The Heaven's declare the Glory of God. Look up.

God has made 400000000000000000000000 (24 zeros) stars! Why worship anyone or anything else?

God invented science.

God invented science. Worship God, not science.

The humble carpenter of Nazareth was also the mighty Architect of the universe.

A sunrise is God's way of telling the world to lighten up.

We should be more concerned with the Rock of Ages, instead of the age of the rocks.

If evolution works, how come mothers still have only 2 hands?

It is not necessary to be in church to be with God.

IX

Faith / Trust

Never will I leave you; never will I forsake you. God Hebrews 13:5

The Lord is the stronghold of my life; of whom shall I be afraid? Psalm 27:1

*Stand firm in the faith; do everything in love.
1 Corinthians 16:13,14*

Fight the good fight of faith. 1 Timothy 6:12

I will fear no evil for you, Lord, are with me. Psalm 23:4

Be strong for I am your God. Joshua 1:9

Without faith it is impossible to please God. Hebrews 11:6

Whoever believes in Jesus will never die. John 11:26

He who believes in Jesus shall live. John 11:25

Be strong - God will go with you. Joshua 1:9

Be courageous for I am with you. God Joshua 1:9

Do not be troubled - trust in God. John 14:1

Fix your eyes on Jesus who perfects your faith. Hebrews 12:2

The Lord is my Rock, my Fortress, my Deliverer. Psalm 18:2

Rejoice in hope; be faithful in prayer. Romans 12:12

Know the hope that God has for you. Ephesians 1:18

Without faith it is impossible to please God. Hebrews 11:6

The righteous are as bold as a lion. Proverbs 28:1

Faith is of greater value than gold. 1 Peter 1:7

Trust in the Lord and He will act. Psalm 37:5

The Lord is good to those whose hope is in Him. Lamentations 3:25

The Lord is my light and my salvation - whom shall I fear? Psalm 27:1

The Lord is the stronghold of my life - of whom shall I be afraid. Psalm 27:1

With God nothing is impossible. Luke 1:37

Never will I leave you; never will I forsake you. Hebrews 13:5

So do not fear for I am with you, do not be dismayed for I am your God. I will strengthen you and help you. I will uphold you with My righteous right hand. Isaiah 41:10

For God did not give us a spirit of fear, but a Spirit of power, of love and of a sound mind. 2 Timothy 1:7

Be confident that He who started a good work in you will complete it. Philippians 1:6

Test Me, says the Lord Almighty and see if I will not pour out My blessings to you. Malachi 3:10

Seek God first and all these things will be added. Matthew 6:33

I am the Lord - those who hope in Me will not be disappointed. Isaiah 49:23

He who belongs to God hears what God says. John 8:47

Fear the loss of faith more than anything.

Goals are dreams with a deadline.

Are you a friend of God on faithbook?

Salvation: don't leave home without it.

Searching for a new look? Have your faith lifted here.

Don't fear - Jesus is near.

I don't doubt your existence. God

Running low on faith? Stop in for a fill-up.

Life is hard - put your trust in God ASAP.

Don't keep the faith - spread it.

Today are you standing on the Promises of God or are you just standing on the floor.

Trust God so we don't have to lie at your funeral.

Change your "worry" into "trust in God".

F E A R = False Evidence Appearing Real.

Fear not - Jesus is with you.

Faith is trusting that God will keep His Word.

Humble people trust in the Lord - the proud don't.

Believe Me now - see Me later. God

The truest end of life is to know that life will never end.

Christians, keep the faith - but not from others.

All wrinkled up with care and worry? It's a good time to get your faith lifted.

Running low on faith? Stop in for a fill-up.

X

Forgiveness

Forgive and you will be forgiven. Luke 6:37

Lord, forgive our sins as we forgive others. Lord's Prayer Matthew 6:12

God will forgive your sins if you ask. 1 John 1:9

Confess sin! God forgives. 1 John 1:9

Though your sins be as scarlet, they shall be as white as snow. Isaiah 1:18

Christian bar of soap: 1 John 1:9 If you confess your sins, He will cleanse you from all unrighteousness.

You confess - Jesus will forgive you. 1 John 1:9

God has a big eraser.

If you're headed in the wrong direction, God allows u-turns.

Get saved from the punishment of your sins. Questions? Call_____

"POBODY'S NERFECT" but Jesus forgives.

Get rid of toxic waste! Forgive.

God brings dead things back to life! R U dead?

Sin stinks - Jesus removes stink!

Forgive to get freedom from anger's hook.

Forgive others as I forgive you! Jesus

If you shower regularly, pray daily for the same reason.

Forgive your enemies - nothing annoys them more.

A believer at war with his brother cannot be at peace with his Father.

When the Devil brings up your past, bring up his future.

Jesus recycles - new earth, new heaven, new life.

People are basically sinful - I can help! Jesus

Nobody is too sinful to be saved.

God deletes corrupt files.

Redemption - God's recycling plan.

Cars are not the only things recalled by their Maker.

Jesus can turn your E F I L around.

Don't live in the prison of sin.

XI

God

I love those who love Me! God Proverbs 8:17

Fear not - I am with you! God Isaiah 41:10

God is our help in trouble. Psalm 46:1

Holy, Holy, Holy, Lord God Almighty. Isaiah 6:3

I am the Lord your God. Leviticus 26:1

Be still and know that I Am God. Psalm 46:10

God is Awesome. Nehemiah 1:5

Don't forget all God's benefits. Psalm 103:2

Never will I leave you; never will I forsake you. God Hebrews 13:5

God is awesome in glory, majestic in holiness. Exodus 15:11

God can make you strong, firm and steadfast. Ask 1 Peter 5:10

God will hold your right hand; fear not. Isaiah 41:13

The Lord is compassionate and gracious. Exodus 34:6

God is in all, over all, and through all. Ephesians 4:6

God is in control. Revelation 19:6

God's telephone # is Jeremiah 33:3: "Call upon me and I will answer."

Everything finds it's purpose in God. Colossians 1:16

Maybe God is testing you to see if you love Him? Deuteronomy 13:3

No God - No Peace: Know God - Know Peace.

The fool says in his heart, "There is no God".

God doesn't need great men - great men need God.

Relax - I am in control. God

Don't reject God because then He will have to reject you.

God is easier to talk to than most Christians.

Without God there would be nothing interesting to do.

If God had a refrigerator, your picture would be on it.

First God tells you, then He enables you, then He empowers you.

Are you a friend of God on Faithbook?

My line is never busy! God

God

When you let God guide, He will provide.

God is at the end of your rope - ask him to help.

A coincidence is when God performs a miracle and decides to remain anonymous.

Those who fear God lack no good thing.

God doesn't call the qualified. He qualifies the called.

Can you prove there is no God?

God grades on the Cross, not the curve.

God is like Tide - He gets stains out others leave behind.

God has no favorites, but He does have intimates.

The highest thought a man can have is a thought of God.

If you love God more than your spouse, you will be married a long time.

God helps the helpless.

I made you and I don't make mistakes! God

I am listening! God

"In God We Trust". The dollar has it correct.

If you doubt God, remember you don't have all the facts.

"Lord God Almighty" is found 57 times in the Bible!

God is awesome - take great joy in knowing Him.

All people have a deep inner sense that God exists.

God is awesome - be thrilled in God.

God Bless America.

America Bless God.

Aim high - seek God hard.

God is almighty! God is all-powerful.

Science is the exploration of God's creation.

God is God, we are not.

God is very, very, very powerful.

Put your trust in God, then give thanks in all circumstances.

Fear God and you won't have anything else to fear.

He who puts God first will be happy at last.

God is Pro-life! Are you?

The bigger God gets to you, the smaller your problems will be.

God made us - God keeps us - God loves us.

If God is small enough to understand, He wouldn't be big enough to worship.

God

Without God, life makes no sense.

God is as close as a "cry for help".

The future is a bright as the Promises of God.

"I AM" means God is in the past, the present and the future.

God wins in the end.

We set the sail - God makes the wind.

God knows you! God loves you! God wants you!

God loves you when everyone else walks away from you.

God is jealous for your devotion.

"G R A C E" is "God's Riches At Christ's Expense".

He who fears God has nothing else to fear.

When God ordains, He sustains.

If you believe there is no God, get ready to meet Him.

XII

Good Works

The horse is made ready for the battle, but the victory belongs to the Lord. Proverbs 21:31

Your work in the Lord in not in vain. 1 Corinthians 15:58

Be ready in season and out of season. 2 Timothy 4:2

It is God who works in you to do His will. Philippians 2:13

Never tire of doing what is right. 2 Thessalonians 3:13

Be rich in good works. 1 Timothy 6:18

God loves a cheerful giver. 2 Corinthians 9:7

Be steadfast, immovable. Give yourselves fully to the work of the Lord. 1 Corinthians 15:58

Bless me and enlarge my territory that Your hand may be upon me and keep me from evil. 1 Chronicles 4:10

It is more blessed to give than receive. Acts 20:35

Good Works

Nothing you do for the Lord is ever useless. 1 Corinthians 15:58

God is able to make all grace abound to you so that in all things, at all times, having all that you need, you will abound in every good work. 2 Corinthians 9:8

Rejoice and be exceedingly glad for great is your reward in Heaven. Matthew 5:11

In trying times don't stop trying.

Our life is our best sermon.

The boy in the Bible that gave up his loaves and fish didn't go hungry.

The fruit is out on the limb.

Do good works! They get help, we get joy, God gets glory.

Are you walking the talk?

Be faithful and fruitful to the finish.

Nothing worth keeping is ever lost in serving God.

Don't spoil the music that God wants to play through you.

When it's impossible, Jesus does his best work.

Let Jesus change your misery into ministry.

Man's disappointments are God's appointments.

No God - No Power: Know God - Know Power.

Love God, love people - nothing else matters.

Be good, be brave, behave.

What you do today matters for eternity.

What is your life counting for?

A Christian is a great "doer" not a great "don'ter".

Be the moon - reflect the Son.

Be a spiritual cheerleader.

You are making a statement by the way you live.

Only one life; will soon be past - only what's done for Christ will last.

What do you do with all the time you save?

May your words to Jesus be "Help" and "Thank You".

Everyone can and must help to carry everyone else.

We never grow to full stature unless we have learned to help someone else.

God owns everything - you are His money manager.

The greatest use of life is to spend it for something that outlasts it.

Nothing worth keeping is lost in serving God.

What we weave in time, we will wear in eternity.

Good Works

Kindness is good to give away because it keeps coming back.

What we do in life echoes in eternity.

One half of the people that have ever lived are alive today. Go and meet someone today.

A dewdrop does the will of God just as much as a thunder storm.

Don't count the things you do - do the things that count.

Love your neighbor as you love yourself.

What are you doing with the rest of your life? God

Failure isn't falling down. It's staying down.

Keep me from diddling my life away Lord.

XIII

Guide

Call upon God - He will answer. Jeremiah 33:3

Jesus Christ is the only way. John 14:6

The Lord is my light and my salvation - whom shall I fear? Psalm 27:1

I will go before you. God Isaiah 45:2

I will instruct you and teach you where you should go. God Psalm 32:8

God will direct you always - just ask. Isaiah 58:11

God will direct your life. Isaiah 58:11

God will lead you beside still waters. Psalm 23:2

God will go before you and make the crooked places straight. Isaiah 45:2

Jesus has a better plan for your life. John 10:10

The Lord is my Shepherd, I shall lack nothing. Psalm 23:1

Ask Me! Jesus Matthew 7:7

Guide

Ask and you will receive. Matthew 7:7

Trust in God and He will direct your path. Proverbs 3:5,6

Jesus is the Way, the Truth, the Life; no one comes to the Father but by Jesus. John 14:6

He who belongs to God hears what God says. 1 John 8:47

Call upon God and He will answer. Jeremiah 33:3

When you let God guide, He will provide.

Google doesn't have all the answers. God

Never loiter on your Heavenly journey - press on.

I am the Way and the Truth. J C

Life is very, very precarious without God.

Lost in life? Let God be your GPS.

Aim high - seek God hard.

God promises a safe landing, not a calm passage.

God is my rock! Shifting sand won't do.

Want to play "Follow the Leader"? Jesus

Heaven is the very best retirement plan.

Jesus is the only one who can give you life happily ever after.

Jesus loves you and has a wonderful plan for your life.

I tell you, my way is best for you! Jesus

"W W J D" What would Jesus do?

Need help? Ask Me! God

Seek Me and you will find Me. God

Jesus came to give you a better life. Don't miss it.

Come, follow Me and I will make you fishers of men. Jesus

Do you have any idea where you are going? God

Need directions? God

If God is with us, who can be against us?

God is as close as a "cry for help".

Need help? I am waiting for you to ask Me. Jesus

Will the road that you are on get you to My place? Jesus

Follow Me! God

XIV

Health

If my people will call upon Me, I will heal their land. God 2 Chronicles 7:14

God heals the brokenhearted and binds up their wounds. Psalm 147:3

Confess your sins so that you may be healed. James 5:16

A cheerful heart is good medicine. Proverbs 17:22

Life without God is frustrating and meaningless. Ephesians 4:17

Come to Me, all you who are weary and carry heavy burdens and I will give you rest. Jesus Matthew 11:28

Crave spiritual food to grow up. 1 Peter 2:2

Praise the Lord Who heals all your diseases. Psalm 103:3

The Lord is able to renew your youth. Psalm 103:5

If you walk in the shadow of death, fear no evil. God is with you. Psalm 23:4

Those who hope in the Lord will renew their strength and not faint. Isaiah 40:31

Church = a hospital for hypocrites.

Achy breaky hearts mended here.

Long lasting relief is not found in a bottle but in the Bible.

Keep your soul healthy. Dr. Jesus

Do you have P. L. O. M. D? "Poor Little Old Me Disease"?

Jesus gets monkeys off people's backs.

Loneliness is being unaware of the One Who is with us everywhere.

Fear or anger problem? Jesus came to set you free.

Pride is the only poison that is good for you when it is swallowed.

God helps the helpless.

I made you and I don't make mistakes. God

Depressed, angry, bored? See Me! Jesus

Don't fear dying, rather fear not having lived.

Feeling down? Just look up! God

Don't fear the future - I am already there. God

Self confidence - good: Christ confidence - best.

Tired? Frustrated? I will give you rest. Jesus

Keep your soul healthy! Jesus MD

Health

Happy are those who seek after God.

Be an organ donor; give your heart to Jesus.

Exercise - love God with all your strength.

Have a spiritual feast! Seek God hard.

God desires you to be happy from the inside out.

Need personal repair? Jesus is a great carpenter.

"KWITCHURBELYAKIN". Give thanks always.

Put on an attitude of gratitude. You will live longer.

Laughter is good medicine. Laugh a lot.

Nothing cooks our goose quicker than a boiling temper.

To stay youthful - stay useful.

Do you have your spiritual seat belt on?

Buckle up spiritually and live.

Make Jesus Christ Lord of your life and live forever.

You can't change the past but you can ruin a perfectly good present by worrying about the future.

Those who are prepared to die, are most prepared to live.

God is Pro-life. Are you?

Rest in the Lord - I will give you rest. Jesus

Everybody is somebody in God's eyes.

The happiest people on earth have their minds focused on Heaven.

Anger doesn't work - try love.

Do you have "hurry" sickness? Wait upon the Lord.

God is at the end of your rope.

The Ten Commandments are your prescription for happiness.

Life without God is intellectually frustrating, useless and meaningless.

Your smile is more important than anything else you wear.

The church is a hospital for sinners, not a rest home for saints.

To look around is to be distressed; to look within is to be depressed; to look up is to be blessed.

What we need in these hectic days is a Christian calmplex.

Fight truth decay - study the Bible daily.

He who angers you controls you.

Too much drama? Allow Jesus into your life.

Tired of living and scared of dying? Try Jesus Christ.

Jesus is my Prozac.

Health

If you can't sleep, don't count sheep. Talk to the Shepherd.

Take two tablets for fast relief - the Ten Commandments.

The best vitamin for a Christian is "B1".

Can't sleep? Try counting your blessings.

A clear conscience makes a soft pillow.

How is your spiritual health? Jesus Christ MD

God loves you too much to leave you the way you are.

Your heart is happiest when it's beating for others.

XV

Heaven

Live in the House of the Lord forever. Psalm 23:6

I shall dwell in the House of the Lord forever. Psalm 23:6

No mind has imagined what God has prepared for those who love Him. 1 Corinthians 2:9

God has promised us eternal life. 1 John 2:25

Eye has not seen what God has prepared for us. 1 Corinthians 2:9

What God has for us in Heaven is fantastic. 1 Corinthians 2:9

The Kingdom of Heaven is near. Matthew 4:17

Precious in the sight of the Lord is the death of His Saints. Psalm 116:15

I, Jesus, go to prepare a mansion for you. John 14:2

Jesus came to give us eternal life. John 3:16

There is life after death. John 3:16

At God's right hand are pleasures for eternity. Psalm 16:11

I will fill you with eternal pleasures. Psalm 16:11

No one can go to Heaven without Christ. John 14:6

The incredible news is that Jesus came to give us eternal life. John 3:16

For Heaven's sake, get saved. John 3:16

God will wipe away every tear in Heaven. Revelation 21:4

I, Jesus, am going to prepare a place for you. 1 John 14

Take hold of eternal life. Go for it. 1 Timothy 6:12

Need eternal fire insurance? Read John 3:16

Want to get ready for Heaven? Jeremiah 33:3

R eady for final exams for Heaven?

You are on Heaven's most wanted list.

When the trumpet sounds, I'm outta here.

If your religion won't take you to church, it is doubtful that it will take you to Heaven.

Hell is the divine stick - Heaven is the divine carrot.

There are no single Christians in Heaven.

Is anything more important than eternity with God?

It appears that there will be more women in Heaven than men. Men - get saved.

Hope springs eternal when the eternal is our hope.

Life has many choices - eternity has two. What's yours?

We can't imagine what God has prepared for those who love Him.

Never loiter on your Heavenly journey - press on.

He who does not make a choice makes a choice.

Is your reservation confirmed? Jesus

I build great homes. God

Heaven - no pain, all gain.

Believe Me now - see Me later.

Heaven - incredible, wonderful, fantastic.

Where will you spend eternity? Smoking or non-smoking?

Are you ready? God

The best reason is "for Heaven's sake".

The weather today in Heaven is absolutely perfect.

Heaven is the very best retirement plan.

Jesus is the only one who can give you life happily ever after.

Heaven

Streets of gold - Welcome! Jesus

Many benefits of being a Christian are out of this world.

Don't be caught dead without Jesus.

What we weave in time, we will wear for eternity.

Three things count for eternity! Location, location, location.

The best opportunity is Heaven. Don't miss it.

Invest in God for the best retirement program.

Future positions eventually opening up in Heaven! Apply within.

Want a trip to Heaven? See salesman inside church for details.

There is only 1 thing you can take with you to Heaven - your kids.
Thanks Awana.

He who puts God first will be happy at last.

Look at your life through Heaven's eyes.

Make Jesus Christ Lord of your life and live forever.

For the Christian, death is just a change of address.

A man may be almost saved yet entirely lost.

Lay up treasure in Heaven.

You can't run with the Devil and expect to reign with the Lord later.

The best is yet to come. God

Your happiest 5 minutes will be your first 5 minutes in Heaven.

Eternity is very long, especially near the end.

Eternal life with Christ is your most valuable possession.

The Godly are designed for inconceivable happiness.

See life in the light of eternity.

The happiest people on earth have their minds focused on Heaven.

Don't miss Heaven for the world.

Heaven is God's great equalizer - He will right all wrongs there.

Wanna walk on streets of gold? Enquire within.

Lay up treasure in Heaven and you will rejoice going there.

At death, we don't leave home, we go home.

It is impossible to exaggerate the joys of Heaven!

Store up treasures in Heaven - it's so safe.

Heaven, not earth, is our home. Plan accordingly.

Treasure: you can't take it with you but you can send it on ahead.

Eternal inexpressible joy! Plan to go there.

The full enjoyment of God is our ultimate home.

Heaven

Judgement Day is coming.

The gift of eternal life has infinite value.

If you died today, would you go to Heaven?

Life has many choices - eternity has two. What's yours?

Heaven is the divine carrot - Hell is the divine stick.

Come, work for the Lord. The hours are long and pay is low but the retirement benefits are out of this world.

The truest end of life is to know that life never ends.

For Heaven's sake!

Rejoice and be exceedingly glad for great is your reward in Heaven.

Hope springs eternal when the eternal is our hope.

Reward or punishment may lie beyond the grave.

Heaven is for real - so is Hell.

A great feast awaits! Jesus

XVI

Hell

Jesus is not willing that any should perish. John 3:16

Jesus came to keep us from the hot spot! John 3:16

Don't get caught with the opposition. God

Every soul winner believes in Hell.

Want to avoid burning? Use Son block.

Turn or burn.

Hell is the divine stick - Heaven is the divine carrot.

Nobody is sent to Hell - people choose Hell.

Life has many choices; eternity has two. What's yours?

He who does not make a choice makes a choice.

Get right or get left.

Hell

Friends don't let friends go to Hell.

Good buddies don't let their buddies go to Hell.

Hell isn't cool. Aim for Heaven.

Those trying to prove there is no Hell, usually have a reason for it.

When the Devil brings up your past, bring up his future.

Looking at the way some people live, they ought to obtain eternal fire insurance soon.

Choose the Bread of Life or you are toast.

To be almost saved is to be totally lost.

Heaven is for real - so is Hell.

You can't run with the Devil and expect to reign with the Lord later.

XVII

Love

———

Love never fails - Jesus loves you. 1 Corinthians 13:8

Love is patient; love does not envy; love does not boast. 1 Corinthians 13:4

Husbands - love your wives. Ephesians 5:25

Live a life of love. Ephesians 5:2

Do everything in love. 1 Corinthians 16:14

Give thanks to the Lord, for He is good; His love endures forever. Psalm 118:1

Stand firm in the faith; do everything in love. 1 Corinthians 16

Love God with all your mind. Matthew 22:37

Love God with all your strength - it's OK. Matthew 22:37

Love God lots. Matthew 22:37

Because you loved God, He will rescue you. Psalm 91:14

God's love is very wide and very deep. Ephesians 3:18

Love

You are My treasured possession. God Deuteronomy 7:6

The Lord is slow to anger and abounding in love. Exodus 34:6

God loved us so much He gave His Son. Believe in Him for eternal life. John 3:16

Be completely humble, bearing with one another in love. Ephesians 4:2

God loves everyone, but prefers "Fruits of the Spirit" over "religious nuts".

If God had a refrigerator, your picture would be on it.

God has no favorites, but He does have intimates.

Make God the great "love of your life".

I love you so much. Jesus

Enjoy the world's buffet but know that God's love tastes the best.

Make enjoying God the passion of your life.

Love the Lord with all your heart - not half.

The best gift you can give your child is to love your spouse.

Love one another! Is that so hard? Jesus

Love your neighbor as yourself. Jesus

"Isle Of View!" Jesus

Love God with ALL your heart.

We are created to be in an intimate love relationship with God.

Loving God is the most important thing you can do today.

Lovers of God always outwork workers of God.

Use the ultimate weapon - deliberate focused Godly love.

Set your goal to have a white hot affection for God.

Love the Lord with all your brains, muscles and heart.

The currency in heaven is "LOVE". Try it here.

Be satisfied with a dissatisfied satisfaction.

Love God; love people - nothing else matters.

Sympathy is two hearts tugging at one load.

Let God be your passion.

God knows you! God loves you! God wants you!

God loves you when everyone else walks away from you.

Heaven is a world of love - choose to go there.

I love you and you and you and you and you. God

God so loved the world that He did not send a committee.

Love

Compassion is difficult to give away because it keeps coming back.

You can give without loving but you cannot love without giving.

Love never fails.

Three things; faith, hope, and love but the greatest of these is love.

XVIII
Prayer

———

Prayer is powerful and effective. James 5:16

The prayer of a Godly person is powerful. James 5:16

Pray continually - don't stop. 1 Thessalonians 5:17

With God nothing is impossible. Luke 1:37

Ask anything in My Name and I will do it. John 14:14

Call upon God; He will answer. Psalm 91:15

Call upon God; He will tell you things you don't know. Jeremiah 33:3

The Lord hears and delivers His from trouble. Psalm 34

Some tears are liquid prayers.

Your Gramma's praying that you'll go to church. Might as well try this church.

"SILENT" and "LISTEN" are the same letters rearranged.

Prayer

Prayer without work is beggary - work without prayer is slavery.

When we depend on man, we get what man can do. When we depend on prayer, we get what God can do.

God's answers are wiser than our prayers.

True prayer is a way of life, not just a case of emergency.

Seven days without prayer make one weak.

You can't imagine the power of prayer.

Power of prayer - free; value of prayer - priceless.

If you are too busy to pray, you are way too busy.

The family that prays together stays together.

A coincidence is when God performs a miracle and decides to remain anonymous.

P U S H - Pray Until Something Happens.

Nobody is saved without prayer.

Try this: No devotions - No breakfast.

Real men pray.

I am listening! God

Life is fragile - handle with prayer.

To hear God's voice - turn down the world's volume.

Pray only on days that end with a "Y".

When praying, don't give God instructions - just report for duty.

Unsatisfied? Try high dosage prayer and Bible meditation.

If you shower regularly, pray daily for the same reason.

Long standing problem? Try kneeling.

Call upon Me and I will answer! God

Prayer is like reverse thunder! God hears it clearly.

Is prayer all it's cracked up to be? Yes, yes, yes, yes, yes, yes.

Let prayer be the key of the day and the bolt of the night.

Prayer may be a thermometer for your love for God.

Why worry when you can pray?

Without prayer, no work is well done.

If you are a stranger to prayer, you are a stranger to power.

Do not face the day until you have faced God.

If trouble drives you to prayer, prayer will drive the trouble away.

More things are accomplished by prayer than the world dreams of.

Prayer

The best way to remember people is in prayer.

Arguments never settle things - but prayer changes things.

No day is well spent without talking to God.

People that do a lot of kneeling don't do a lot of lying.

Are you too busy to pray? Jesus

There are 3 answers to prayer: Yes, No, or Wait awhile.

Daily prayers lessen daily cares.

Prayerlessness results in carelessness.

You have a chance to make a difference - do it!

Listen to no man who has not listened to God.

Pray carefully - God always answers.

Prayer is a disinfectant and a preventative.

Prayer is powerful.

Worry is 'upside down prayer'.

To work is to pray and to pray is to work - Oralabora.

Why worry when you can pray?

When it seems the hardest to pray, we should pray the hardest.

God is easier to talk to than most people.

Anything worth worrying about, is worth praying about.

Prayer will either make a man stop sinning or sin will make him stop praying.

People who do not believe in prayer will generally make an exception when tragedy strikes.

Life is fragile - handle with prayer.

It should not be uncommon to hear God's voice.

God is jealous for your devotion.

"PRAY" is a four letter word that you can use anywhere.

Turn your heart into a prayer factory.

Unused prayer looks like anxiety.

A day hemmed in with prayer rarely unravels.

God answers knee-mail.

He who kneels before God, can stand before anyone.

Courage is fear that has said it's prayers.

No time to pray makes you easy prey.

We need to talk! God

Prayer

Fifty percent of sick persons need prayer more than pills, aspirations more than aspirins, meditation more than medicine.

As long as there are tests, there will be prayer in public schools.

This church is prayer-conditioned.

It's hard to stumble when you are down on your knees.

Lack of prayer looks like anxiety - God answers knee mail.

XIX
Problems-Tasks

——

All things work together for good for those who love the Lord. Romans 8:28

For our light and momentary troubles are achieving for us an eternal glory. 2 Corinthians 4:17

All-surpassing power is available to you from God. 2 Corinthians 4:7

God's power is made perfect in our weakness. 2 Corinthians 12:9

God's strength will help you in trouble. Psalm 46:1

Is there anything too hard for the Lord? No! Genesis 18:14

Be strong and courageous for the Lord your God will go with you. Joshua 1:9

Do not be depressed or terrified for the Lord your God will go with you. Joshua 1:9

The Lord your God will fight for you. Deuteronomy 1:30

The Lord is a refuge for those who trust in Him. Nahum 1:7

Ask and you will receive. Matthew 7:7

Call upon God and He will deliver you. Psalm 50:15

When God has tested me, I will come out as gold. Job 23:10

Walking in the valley of death? Fear not; God is with you. Psalm 23:4

My God shall supply all your needs. Philippians 4:13

Cast your concerns on God - He will sustain you. Psalm 55:22

Cast your troubles on the Lord - He will help. Psalm 55:22

In your day of trouble, God will answer you. Psalm 86:7

Troubles? God delivers you from them. Psalm 34:19

In everything give thanks. 1 Thessalonians 5:18

Suffering makes us bitter or better. Maybe God is testing you to see if you love Him? Deuteronomy 13:3

For the Christian, suffering has meaning. Romans 5:3

Be brave, I am with you always! God Joshua 1:9

Maybe God is testing you to see if you love Him? Deuteronomy 13:3

Ready for final exams for Heaven?

Jonah learned more in the fish than many learn in seminary.

Life is like an onion - you peel off one layer at a time and sometimes you weep.

God chooses ordinary people to do extraordinary jobs.

God gives every bird it's food, but He does not throw it into his nest.

Worry = stewing without doing.

Clouds in our lives are sent many times to bring showers of blessings.

The task ahead of us is never as great as the Power behind us.

You can tell how big a person is by what it takes to discourage him.

God uses suffering - don't waste it.

God uses us the most when we are the weakest.

Modern culture is trying to mix all religions into one.

Worry is the dark room where negatives are developed.

Suffering may exist to help you love God more.

Tell your problems how big God is.

With God nothing is impossible! Go "Vikings".

Alone you can't - together We can! God

Christianity answers the "Why" question.

God is over all, in all and through all.

God whispers to us in our prosperity. He shouts to us in our calamity.

Problems-Tasks

There will be trials - better get to know Jesus.

I have a purpose behind every one of your problems. God

Trouble is faith's finest hour.

Sometimes it takes a painful situation to make us change our ways.

God uses our down times to build us up.

People who do not believe in prayer will generally make an exception when tragedy strikes.

A little engine trouble during an airplane flight can reach more souls than a good preacher in a pulpit.

Be sure - if God sends you on a stony path, He will provide you with strong shoes.

God is trying hard to get your attention.

When down in the mouth, remember Jonah. He came out all right.

Don't give up. Moses was once a basket case.

Jesus came to get you out of serious trouble.

Grief may come your way to test your faith.

The dark threads are as needful in the weaver's skillful hand, as the threads of gold and silver in the pattern He has planned.

Christians are like tea - their strength is not drawn out until they get in hot water.

God promises a safe landing, not a calm passage.

God is in the end - don't jump ship.

XX

Temptation

The Lord knows how to rescue Godly men from trials. 2 Peter 2:9

Do not steal. Exodus 20:15

Do not lie. Exodus 20:16

God knows your thoughts. Matthew 11:21

Do not envy. Exodus 20:17

Satan is trying to steal, kill and destroy you. John 10:10

Tempted? Flee like Joseph did. Genesis 39:12

Flee youthful lusts. 2 Timothy 2:22

Stuffed hidden sin rots the bones. Psalm 32

E very temptation is an opportunity to flee to God.

Lord, grant me patience - but hurry.

Sin always starts out as being fun.

It is unlikely that there will be a reduction in the wages of sin.

Don't forfeit eternal rewards for temporary gain now.

Pride grows like weeds - weed often.

God uses us the most when we are the weakest.

Sin is the insanity of seeking pleasure outside of God's will.

Sin never stands still - it always continues to grow.

Enjoy the world's buffet but know that God's love tastes the best.

it takes a very strong person to say "No".

Every day is Judgement Day - use a lot of it.

Flee from sin - it always hurts too much.

Get right or get left.

Sin stinks - Jesus removes stink.

It costs a lot more to say "No" to God than to say "Yes".

If Christ is kept outside, something must be wrong inside.

God knows your thoughts! Keep'm pure.

God's absolutes are absolutely absolute.

If it's wrong, don't do it for Heaven's sake.

Temptation

God is very, very, very powerful.

Jesus is coming back - don't miss Him for the world.

Someone has figured that we have thirty five thousand laws trying to enforce the Ten Commandments.

The path of the world seems pleasant enough if you don't stop to think where you're going.

The most expensive thing in the world is sin.

The Devil gratifies; God satisfies.

Christ is not sweet until sin is made bitter to us.

Disregard for God is the greatest evil in the west today.

Sin is irrational - it eventually always hurts us so badly.

Five deadly sins - pride, anger, gluttony, lust, and apathy.

If its too important to give up, it's too important to have.

Deal ruthlessly with sin. See Me! Jesus

Two main enemies of the spiritual life; anger and greed.

God is testing you! Do well.

Never postpone obedience to Jesus.

Greatly fear to offend God!

Pride can just about ruin anything.

There is no worse slavery than slavery to sin.

If Christ is kept outside, something must be wrong inside.

Christians are not sinless, but they should sin less.

If a sermon pricks your conscience, it must have some good points.

EGO = "Easing God Out".

Dusty Bibles lead to dirty lives.

Try "moral beautification". Jesus will help you.

Get rid of 'stinking thinking'. Keep your thoughts pure.

What part of "Thou shall not" don't you understand?

If you don't want to reap the fruits of sin, stay out of the Devil's orchard.

Temptations are like bums - treat one nice and he will return with many of his friends.

Keep me from diddling my life away Lord.

If it's wrong - don't do it! Bible.

Give Satan an inch and he will become a ruler.

Don't live in the prison of sin.

XXI
Wealth

———

Whoever has money never has enough money. Ecclesiastes 5:10

True wealth consists of being rich toward God. 2 Corinthians 6:10

True Christians own nothing but possess everything. 2 Corinthians 6:10

What we give determines our wealth, not what we get.

A good place for the "buck to stop" is at the offering plate.

Plenty of people give God credit - few give Him cash.

No man is poor who has a Godly mother.

It is unlikely that there will be a reduction in the wages of sin.

There is infinite value in knowing Jesus Christ as Lord.

Contentment with Godliness makes you a very rich person.

Contentment with Godliness is great gain.

Salvation is free but not valid until you ask for it.

Want to be rich? Count your many blessings.

Stingy Christians should be an extinct species.

Jesus invested His life in you! Any interest yet?

You are a very poor person if you have to pay for your sins.

If God charged you $25 for each of your sins, how much money would you owe Him?

No one can serve 2 masters; choose to love God more than money.

You can be rich and yet very poor. Be rich in God.

Whatever is given to God is touched by immortality.

Giving is the only antidote to materialism.

Lay up treasure in Heaven and you will rejoice going there.

Keep poor in things and keep rich in God.

If it's too important to give up, it's too important to have.

Satan wants you to accumulate, accumulate, accumulate.

Do you have a possession obsession?

God owns everything - you are His money manager.

All your possessions are on loan to you from God.

Wealth

When it comes to giving, some people stop at nothing.

Treasure: you can't take it with you but you can send it on ahead.

Where your treasure is, there your heart shall be also.

Giving is the best way of living.

Do you tithe as much as you tip?

Do your givin' while you'r liven so you'r knowin' where it's goin'.

No matter which way the market is moving, God is always better than gold.

It costs nothing to become a Christian but it costs everything to be a Christian.

Discontent makes rich men poor, while contentment makes poor men rich.

He is richest who has few wants.

You can give without loving but you can't love without giving.

Your faith has much greater value than gold.

Don't spend your health to gain wealth, and then spend your wealth to regain your health.

Make God your greatest treasure.

Tithe if you love Jesus! Anyone can honk.

Give God what's right - not what's left.

Live to give - not get.

Born-Selfish; Born Again-Generous.

XXII

Holidays

Christmas

———

Christ came to proclaim freedom. Luke 4:10

Good News of great joy for all people. Luke 2:10

Happy Birthday Jesus! Merry Christmas

Supernatural love story! Jesus Christ - Merry Christmas.

The greatest gift is Jesus Christ! Merry Christmas

"MERRY___MAS" It's just not the same without CHRIST.

The most important part of "CHRISTMAS" is the 1st 6 letters.

What would happen if God came down and lived with us?

"Immanuel" = Jesus Christ God with us.

Feel the Christmas spirit all year long - become a Christian.

Jesus Christ - a Gift too wonderful for words.

Jesus Christ - totally God and totally man. Merry Christmas

Jesus is the Reason for the Season.

There was no room in the inn - do you have room for Jesus?

The inn keeper didn't know it was Christ! Do you know Christ?

Glory to God in the highest, on earth peace to men.

The greatest Gift! Jesus Christ Merry Christmas

Celebrate the King! December 25

God gave Jesus; Jesus gave His life! Merry Christmas

Wise men still seek Jesus.

Come in and pray today. Beat the Christmas rush.

EASTER
Don't be troubled, trust in Jesus. John 14:1

Jesus Christ died to take our sins away. 1 Peter 3:18 Happy Easter

I have risen and I shall return soon. Jesus Christ

Jesus loves you! Easter proves it.

Forgive others as I forgive you! Jesus

Jesus built a bridge with 2 boards and 3 nails! Happy Easter

Jesus paid a bill He didn't owe! Happy Easter

Need help? Reach for the nail scarred hand.

I have risen and I shall return soon! Jesus Christ

Jesus Christ proved it all with 3 nails! Happy Easter

Three nails didn't hold Jesus on the Cross. Love did! Happy Easter

1 Cross + 3 Nails = 4 given!

The best mathematical equation I have ever seen: 1 Cross + 3 Nails = 4 given.

People use duct tape to fix everything; God used 3 nails! Happy Easter.

Jesus Christ is risen indeed! Happy Easter

Jesus rose from the dead and was seen by family and friends multiple times for 40 days.

After Christ rose from the dead, 500 people saw him over 40 days.

Easter - Jesus Christ is the offer - deal or no deal?

Jesus' tomb - empty; He is risen.

Christ Jesus died to bring us to God.

Jesus rose from the dead - we also will rise after death.

I am making Heaven for you! Jesus Happy Easter

I make happy endings! Jesus Happy Easter

Jesus died and rose from the dead proving that He is God!

Jesus Christ's tomb's empty! He is risen indeed!

After death, there will be life! Jesus

Pilate was really the person on trial.

What are you doing with Jesus this Easter?

Live for Jesus - He died for you.

Do I need to die for you before you will listen? Jesus

Give sin up for Lent! You'll be so happy.

The Easter Story = Supernatural Love.

On the back of Satan's neck, there is a nail-scarred footprint.

News you can use: He hung for your hang ups.

Buddha's tomb - occupied. Mohammed's tomb - occupied. Jesus' tomb - empty! Why follow a loser?

FISHING SEASON
Fish with Jesus - you catch'm, He'll clean'm.

Jesus was a great fisherman.

I will make you fishers of men! Jesus

Fishing is great in Heaven.

The best day fishing is nothing compared to any day in Heaven.

Even a fish stays out of trouble if he keeps his mouth shut.

A woman who has never seen her husband fishing doesn't know what a patient man she married.

Never open a can of worms unless you want to go fishing.

Even Jesus had a fish story.

THANKSGIVING
Thank you, thank you, thank you, thank you God! Happy Thanksgiving

Give thanks in all circumstances! Happy Thanksgiving.

Every day should be Thanksgiving.

Thanksgiving is good but "THANKSLIVING" is better.

Jesus Christ is the answer to all your needs! Happy Thanksgiving

Worried? Then pray. Afraid? Then pray. Happy? Give thanks!

MOTHER'S/FATHER'S DAY
Honor your Father and Mother - you will live longer. Ephesians 6:1

Mom - We love you! Happy Mom's Day

Dad - We love you! Happy Dad's Day

Everyday is "Heavenly Father Day."

Our Father in Heaven; Your will be done! Lord's Prayer

NEW YEAR
What does God require? Act justly, love mercy, walk humbly. Micah 6:8
Happy New Year

Need directions in the New Year? Lets Talk! God

Do unto others as you would have them do to you. Happy New Year

I am the only one who really knows about the New Year. God

Planning for your future? I am! God

We can't imagine what God has prepared for those who love Him.

VALENTINE'S DAY
Husbands, love your wives. Ephesians 6

Valentine Week - Love God the most.

They will know you are a Christian by your love.

Love your neighbor as you love yourself.

Do unto others as you would have them do unto you.

Love God; love others! The two big Commandments.

MEMORIAL DAY
Put on the Armor Of God. Ephesians 6

We salute you who have served our country! Happy Memorial Weekend

The best freedom is freedom in Christ.

The greatest love is to give your life for another.

SPRING
Hello Spring - goodby Seasonal affective disorder.

April showers bring May flowers.

Clocks - Spring forward. Fall back in November.

4TH OF JULY
Christ came to proclaim freedom. Luke 4:10

God's fireworks are out of this world. Happy 4th

Christ came to set the captives free! Are you free?

Pray that your devotions will be like the last 20 seconds of the fireworks display.

God's lightning and thunder are greater than the fireworks display.

HALLOWEEN
Seek the Overcomer, not the Undertaker. Happy Halloween

Life can be scary - Help Lord!

Don't fear dying - fear having not lived.

The real "Comforter" is the Holy Spirit.

Fear not for I am with you. Jesus

Have no anxiety about anything - try prayer.

LABOR DAY
Come if you labor hard and I will give you rest. Matthew 11:28

Your labor in the Lord is not in vain. 1 Corinthians 15:58

Give yourself fully to the work of the Lord. Happy Labor Day

Work, for the night is coming.

Be like God - work 6 days, then rest.

ELECTIONS
Pray - then Vote - then Pray!

XXIII

The Devil

Resist the Devil and he will flee from you. James 4:7

Satan comes to destroy your wealth, your health, and your relationships. John 10:10

True Christians are Satan Crushers.

Jesus Christ came to destroy the works of Satan.

Satan trembles when he sees the weakest Christian on his knees.

Christians are Satan's worst nightmare.

Turn or burn.

Resist the Devil - submit to his enemy.

The Devil promises you the whole world, but he doesn't own a grain of sand.

The Devil will extend plenty of credit, but think of the payment.

On the back of Satan's neck, there is a nail-scarred footprint.

The Devil is not afraid of a dust covered Bible.

The Devil is never too busy to rock the cradle of a backslider.

Try Jesus. If you don't like Him, the Devil will always take you back.

Satan is fishing for suckers - don't get hooked on his bait.

Temptations are like bums. Treat one nice and he will return with many of his friends.

Never give the Devil a ride. He always wants to drive.

Satan subtracts and divides. God multiplies and multiplies.

Give Satan an inch and he'll be a ruler.

You can't run with the Devil and expect to reign with the Lord later.

The Devil gratifies - God satisfies.

When the Devil brings up your past, bring up his future.

If you do not want to reap the fruits of sin, stay out of the Devil's orchard.

XXIV

Jokes/Riddles

—

Laugh a lot and when you are older all your wrinkles will be in the right places.

Eve's phone number in the Garden of Eden? ADAM 812

Which Bible character had no parents? Joshua, Son of Nun

What kind of man was Boaz before he married? Ruthless

Who was the most successful doctor in the Bible? Job - He had the most patience.

What did the cat say when the Ark landed? Is that Ararat?

What did Noah say as he was loading the Ark? "Now I herd everything".

What animal could Noah not trust? The Cheetah

Dear Mom and Dad; Gue$$ what I need? Plea$e $end $ome $oon.
   Love, Your $on

Son: Dad, how soon will I be old enough to do as I please?
Father: I don't know; nobody has lived that long yet!

What do you call a person who is crazy about money? A Doughnut

Sometimes I wake up grumpy - other days I let him sleep.

Only the baker can make dough and loaf.

Why was 10 so sad? Because 7 8 9.

What did the #0 say to the #8? Nice belt you have there.

Have you ever seen a Man-eating fish? Yes, in a seafood restaurant.

How do you stop a fish from smelling? Hold it's nose.

Who serves the Pope his potato chips? The Chipmonks

What did the boy Octopus say to the girl Octopus? I want to hold your hand, hand, hand, hand, hand, hand. hand, hand.

Who performs operations at the Fish Hospital? The Head Sturgeon

How do you get dragon milk? From a cow with short legs.

How do you make an Elephant fly? First get a great big zipper.

Corduroy pillows: they're making headlines.

Did you hear about the tree surgeon who fell out of his patient?

What do you call a pig that knows karate? A Pork Chop

What do you call a grizzly without teeth? A Gummy Bear

I wondered why the baseball was getting bigger. Then it hit me.

Police were called to a daycare where a three year old was resisting a rest.

Did you hear about the guy whose whole left side was cut off? He's all right now.

The roundest knight at King Arthur's Round Table was Sir Cumference.

When fish are in schools they sometimes take debate.

A thief who stole a calendar got twelve months.

A thief fell and broke his leg in wet cement. He became a hardened criminal.

Insanity is hereditary; you get it from your kids.

We'll never run out of math teachers because they are always multiplying.

Cats are just tiny women in fur coats.

Why is it hard to have a conversation with a goat? Because it's always butting in.

What athlete can jump higher than a building? Any athlete - buildings can't jump.

What do Dentists call their X-rays? Tooth Pics

What is at the end of everything? The letter "G"

What did the mother buffalo say to her son before he left? Bison

Why is basketball a messy sport? Because the players dribble all over the court.

What kind of flowers grow between your nose and your chin? Tulips

Why did the pony have a sore throat? Because it was a little horse.

You are stuck with your debt if you can't budge it.

A lot of money is 'tainted'-'taint yours and 'taint mine.

A boiled egg is hard to beat.

Those who get too big for their britches will be exposed in the end.

When she saw her first strands of gray hair, she thought she'd dye.

Ever hear about Irish Alzheimer's Disease? You forget about everything but your grudge.

Why couldn't they play cards on the Ark? Noah was sitting on the deck.

Was Noah the first one out of the Ark? No, he came fourth out of the Ark.

Where did Noah keep the bees? In the Ark hives.

Why couldn't Noah catch many fish? He only had two worms.

What is a small joke called? A "mini-ha ha"